START-UP
VS
ENTREPRENEURSHIP

We are here again as those who rebelled against the usual system. Dear reader, we not only share our articles with you, but also have similar feelings. However, we must work hard and start living the lives we dream of instead of envying them. For this, it takes a lot of work.

As the say..

"... At least you will know
three languages
at least in three languages
At least three languages
Because you are neither
history nor geography
What are you, what are you
My son Mernus
You are the child of a nation
that missed the bus.

... "

Today, Start-Up vs. We will talk about entrepreneurship.

What is Entrepreneurship?

To explain in the simplest terms, the concept we call entrepreneurship is to establish a completely profit-oriented business by taking some risks. It's not like innovation. Launching a new idea or product is not an unexpected situation here.

For example, you are considering opening a restaurant near a plaza. Your expectation is to attract plaza employees or other customers to your restaurant and try to impress them with your taste. However, if we need to look at it from a more general perspective, this is a problem with a solution and you become a business established for profit in a circulation in line with the needs of people in daily life.

WHAT IS START-UP?

The concept we call Start-Up is the name given to startups that use all technological opportunities to produce a solution for a problem that has no solution and develop ideas, products or services with extensive R&D studies.

When we look at the meaning of the word, start-up appears in the form of "starting". In fact, when we look at it as a meaning, it has a very good meaning. Because it is used for companies that start from scratch and develop and grow. Starting from scratch or "Start-up" does not mean zero capital. Such companies start from scratch in terms of the service they will produce or offer.

What is the Difference Between Entrepreneurship and Start-Up?

Start-Ups and normal companies actually follow different paths from each other. Start-Ups are not like regular companies. Start-Ups are temporary companies. "What does temp company mean? Are we scammers?" Let's briefly define it without any questions such as: 😊 There is a clear main idea in the establishment of temporary companies.

When the problem is solved with a product, service or technology, it means the end of the start-up (temporary) company. Because such companies work to find out what needs to be produced rather than producing. They can market the solutions they find to other companies, or they can switch from a temporary company position to a regular company if they trust the solution they find and want to continue.

Start-Ups are a kind of transition phase between Normal and permanent companies. The reason why it is temporary is due to the goal of finding a solution to a problem they have determined within a certain period of time. What if they can't find a solution? That's where they don't get stubborn and accept their failures and end the Start-Up.

Let's say you have the idea of Start-Up and you want to implement it, let's answer the question in your mind immediately...

How to Install Start-Up?

Setting up a Start-Up means going step by step. Since the development of Start-Up-style companies is accelerated, you need to create your roadmap beforehand in order to keep up with this rapid acceleration.

The key point here should not be to save the moment, you should always think about the future by considering all the parameters, conditions and possibilities. This type of company wants permanent solutions. And you should do a wide range of studies on how the problem you found will evolve in the future.

Well Then...

How to Grow a Start-Up?

1.

Filter and Question Existing Methods

The methods applied by other companies can be a guide for you. However, remember that your target audience may not be the same.

If you are faced with such a situation, you may not be able to reach your goal because your project is directed to the wrong method and target audience. Market research, R&D studies and target audience studies are of great importance here.

2.

Don't Try Multiple Concurrent Supply Channels

It means picking yourself up from one place and throwing it to another, simultaneous supply channel. As tempting as the idea of trying a little bit of everything may seem tempting at first glance, it's the same as shooting yourself in the foot.

What is needed to gain experience is actually time. Trying out more than one supply channel while you're still in the early stages and don't have much experience can make it difficult to decide which supply channel to opt out.

3.

Scale Up

We can consider scaling as a must-have to see how your company is going. You can create scalings and instructions in your roadmap, which you will follow, by putting them under the right metrics.

4.

Focus on a Small Niche Market

Who you want to work with is very important at this point. The people or institutions you work with, 80% of your time is spent on customers trying to figure out what to do.

It must be a pity that the concept of "time", which we think should not be compromised for the age we belong to, is used so much. By getting the right customer, you can save time and continue to add experience to your experience quickly.

5.

Identify Your Target Audience

Without your target audience, this business will never work. You make random sales and fluctuations will meet you when you make a table of sales you make.

One of the most important issues in increasing your graphics exponentially is to determine the target audience correctly and to produce solutions for the needs of the target audience. You should define your target audiences in a specific way.

For example; The more you keep your age scale apart, the further away you get from the inner world, needs and interests of your potential customers. You can accelerate your sales by understanding the needs of your customers, producing customer-oriented products, determining their demographic characteristics, and arranging marketing messages according to their target audience.

Dear readers, in this article, we wanted to give you as much information as possible about the differences between Start-Up and entrepreneurship and a possible Start-Up action. We hope that we have been able to shine a light on each of you. Don't be the one to shoot your feet!